ELEPHANTS

THE WILDLIFE IN DANGER SERIES

Louise Martin

Rourke Enterprises, Inc.
Vero Beach, Florida 32964

LIBRARY OF CONGRESS
Library of Congress Cataloging-in-Publication Data

Martin, Louise, 1955-
  Elephants / by Louise Martin.

    p. cm. — (Wildlife in danger)
    Includes index.
    Summary: Describes the two remaining species of
elephants, the African and the Asiatic, and how these
animals are struggling against both man and nature for
their survival.
    ISBN 0-86592-998-X
    1. Elephants — Juvenile literature.   2. Endangered
species — Juvenile literature.   3. Wildlife conservation —
Juvenile literature.   [1. Elephants.   2.Rare animals
3.Wildlife conservation]   I. Title.   II. Series:
Martin, Louise, 1955-
Wildlife in danger.
QL737.P98M37   1988
639.9'7961 - dc19   88-10317
                                          CIP
                                          AC

*Title page photo: Asiatic
elephant (Elephas maximu*

TABLE OF CONTENTS

ELEPHANTS

Elephants are the largest land mammals in the world. Although there used to be many kinds of elephants, today there are only two. African elephants *(Loxodonta africana)* are the larger of the two **species**. They can easily be recognized by their huge, flapping ears. Asiatic elephants *(Elephas maximus)*, also called Indian elephants, are not so big, and their ears are much smaller.

African elephants have huge ears

WHERE THEY LIVE

As their names suggest, African elephants live in Africa, and Asiatic elephants live in Asia. African elephants used to be common in all parts of Africa south of the Sahara Desert. Today there are not nearly so many. There are also fewer Asiatic elephants now. The largest population of Asiatic elephants is found in India, where there are probably over 20,000. Many of these are used as work elephants. They help people drag heavy loads through the jungle where machines cannot go.

Asiatic elephants help people in the forests

THREATS TO ELEPHANTS

Like so many animals, elephants are struggling against both humans and nature for their survival. People are destroying the forests where the Asiatic elephants live and killing the African elephants for their **ivory tusks**. Nature brings droughts to Africa and destroys the elephants' feeding grounds. Of the two threats to the elephants' survival, humans are by far the greater menace.

Elephants live in forests like this

HUNTING ELEPHANTS

  For thousands of years, people hunted elephants for their ivory tusks. Early this century, an estimated 100,000 elephants were killed each year for that reason. In most countries today, the trade in ivory is controlled by the government of that country. Only a certain number of elephants can be killed each year. Ivory, like gold and jewels, is worth a very high price. The elephants' main enemies are **poachers**, people who kill animals illegally, without permission from the government. They take the tusks only and sell them illegally.

*An African elephant with its ivory
tusks*

An Indian elephant feeding

Elephants use their tusks and trunks to eat

ELEPHANTS AND FARMERS

Elephants also have to compete with humans for land. In Asia, people are destroying the woods and forests where the elephants live to make room for farms. Elephants are messy eaters. They crash through the forests, knocking over the trees and destroying more than they eat. If a farmer sees an elephant straying onto his farm, he may shoot it to stop it from spoiling his crops. To protect elephants from farmers and from poachers, many have been put into nature reserves.

A female elephant with her bab

SEARCHING FOR FOOD

Elephants have huge appetites. Fully grown elephants eat four to five hundred pounds of grass, leaves, fruit, and tree bark each day. The herds move from one place to another looking for food and water. They destroy the **vegetation** in one area and move on to another to find food. In the nature reserves, elephants do not have as much room to move around. They keep returning to feeding places before the vegetation has recovered and is ready to eat. Often, they cannot find enough to eat.

An elephant digs for water in a dried-up river bed

BABY ELEPHANTS

Scientists have found that elephants who do not have enough to eat take longer to grow to adult size. This means that female elephants often do not have **calves** until they are about eighteen years old. Elephants normally have a calf every four years, but now, many only have the strength to have one calf every eight years. Scientists are studying ways of making sure elephants in the reserves eat well. Then they will be strong enough to produce healthy calves to continue the species.

Elephants can live safely on the nature reserves

ELEPHANTS NEED WATER

Elephants need about thirty gallons of water each day. They drink it and use it to keep themselves cool in the hot African or Indian sun. Elephants can draw up a gallon and a half of water in their trunks at one time. They spray the water over their ears and bodies and into their mouths. In times of **drought**, or dry periods, elephants have to dig for water in dried-up river beds. They scoop out the dried earth with their two forefeet until they reach water below.

An African bull elephant charge across the savannah

148

HOW WE CAN HELP

Long ago, elephants had no trouble finding enough food and water. But then human beings began to change the natural balance in both the African savannah and the forests of Asia. Now humans are trying to restore places for the elephants to live. The forests will never grow back to their former size, but large animal reserves can almost take their place. There, elephants can live, well-fed and safe from poachers.

Glossary

calf (KAV) - a baby elephant

drought (drowt) - a water shortage due to lack of rainfall

ivory tusk (IVE or ee TUSK) - long teeth that stick out from each
   side of an elephant's mouth, made of a kind of bone

poachers (POE churz) - people who hunt animals without
   permission

species (SPE seez) - a scientific term meaning kind or type

vegetation (ve ge TAY shun) - a collective name for plants
   and trees

INDEX